Animals in Fall

by Melvin and Gilda Berger

SCHOLASTIC INC.

ISBN 978-0-545-47649-2

12 11 10 9   18 19 20 21

Printed in the U.S.A.   40
First printing, October 2012

Photo Credits: Photo Research: Alan Gottlieb

Photos ©: cover: Margaret M Stewart/Shutterstock; back cover: Rolf Nussbaumer/Nature Picture Library; 1: Foxtrot101/
Shutterstock; 3: Accent Alaska.com/Alamy Images; 4: Brad Whitsitt/Shutterstock; 5: Thomas & Pat Leeson/Science
Source; 6: Bob Stefko/Getty Images; 7: David Kjaer/Nature Picture Library; 8: Lisa Moore/Alamy Images; 9: Austin
J. Stevens/Animals Animals; 10: Pablo77/Shutterstock; 11: Dorling Kindersley/Getty Images; 12: Rusty Dod-son/
Shutterstock; 13: Gerold & Cynthia Merker/Visuals Unlimited, Inc.; 14: Tom Walker/Visuals Unlimited, Inc.; 15: mirceax/
Thinkstock; 16: Phillip W. Kirkland/Shutterstock.

What do animals do in fall?

Squirrels get ready for winter.

Does the squirrel have a bushy tail?

They bury nuts.

Geese get ready for winter.

Are the geese flying in a line?

They fly south.

Frogs get ready for winter.

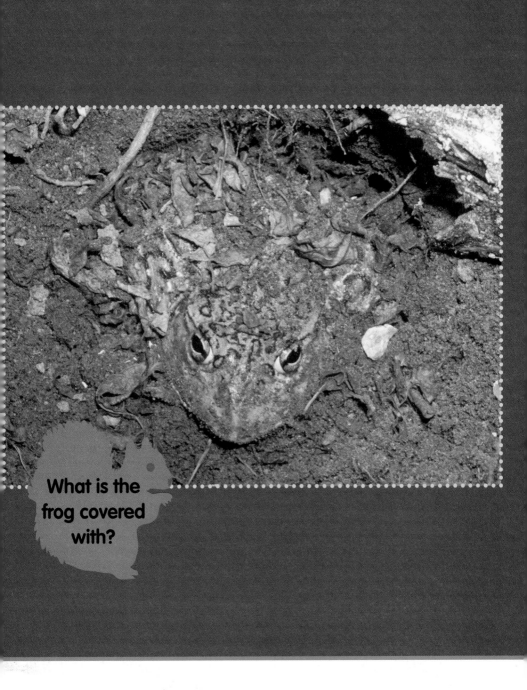

What is the frog covered with?

They hide underground.

Bears get ready for winter.

They go to sleep.

Is the snake on brown leaves?

Snakes get ready for winter.

They crawl under rocks.

Foxes get ready for winter.

Some change color.

sk Yourself

1. What do squirrels do in fall?
2. Where do geese fly for winter?
3. How do frogs keep warm in winter?
4. What do bears do in winter?
5. Do some foxes change color
   for winter?

You can find the answers in this book.